St   lege

COMICS AND MAGAZINES

Tim Merrison

MEDIA STORY

MEDIA STORY

ADVERTISING

BOOKS

COMICS AND MAGAZINES

FILMS

PLAYS

TV AND VIDEO

Series Designer: Helen White
Editors: Kate Haycock and Jim Kerr

Cover: A cover from 'The Real Ghostbusters'.

First published in 1990 by
Wayland (Publishers) Ltd
61 Western Road, Hove
East Sussex BN3 1JD

Phototypeset by Direct Image Photosetting Ltd., Hove, Sussex, England
Printed in Italy by G. Canale & C.S.p.A.
Bound in Portsmouth by MacLehose

British Library Cataloguing in Publication Data
Merrison, Tim
Comics and magazines.
1. Comics   2. Magazines
I. Title   II. Series
741.5

ISBN 1-85210-990-4

CONTENTS

WHAT ARE COMICS AND MAGAZINES?

TAKE A look at yourself in the mirror. You may not realize it, but you are a very important person! Your likes and dislikes are of great interest. You have power!

Do you recognize this description of yourself? You should! To prove it, you only have to walk into any newsagent's shop and you will see at least one whole shelf filled with magazines and comics aimed just at you, the 'pre-teenage' reader.

Children looking at the American comic 'Dick Tracy Weekly'.

Why are you so special? The answer is simple. You have spending power! Each week hundreds of thousands of boys and girls like you spend a total of over one million pounds on their favourite comics and magazines.

Comics and magazines are very different from each other. Comics deal with a cartoon world of fun and adventure. Magazines, however, are much more concerned with the 'real world' and what you find interesting and exciting about it. They have fashions you want to wear, music you prefer to listen to and television

Typical features in children's magazines are interviews with TV stars, like the actresses in 'Neighbours', and pop stars.

programmes you love to watch. So, it is very important that the people who produce these comics and magazines know what you think, feel and want.

Have you ever wondered how your favourite magazines and comics are put together? How are they planned? How are they produced? Who makes sure they are delivered to shops on time? Here is your chance to find out!

PLANNING A MAGAZINE

MAGAZINES DEAL with both general and special interests. Most of them take a light-hearted approach to a whole range of subjects, from sport to pop music. They are bright and colourful, fun to look at and fun to read. And, if they hit the right note with their audience, they can be very popular.

These children are looking at pictures of basketball stars Michael Jordan and Larry Bird.

Each issue of a magazine has to be planned, **researched**, written, **designed**, printed and sent out to shops. If you look carefully through your favourite magazine, you will find a list of the people who have produced the latest issue. Usually this list will be at the bottom of the contents page or inside the back cover.

You will notice that the people who work for the magazine are divided into three major departments – the editorial, advertising and **marketing** departments. The editorial department is responsible for writing and designing each issue. The advertising department tries to persuade as many businesses as possible to place advertisements (adverts) in the magazine. The marketing department looks for ways to attract new readers and makes sure that the magazine keeps in touch with the wishes and needs of its readers.

The planning meeting
The first stage in producing a magazine is the planning meeting. This is where all the members of the editorial team meet to discuss the contents of the next issue. A large magazine has one editor who is in charge of other editors. Each of these editors controls one particular area of the magazine, for example news features, personal computer games, pop music or fashion.

At the planning meeting, each editor puts forward ideas for interesting articles and features. Many of these ideas come from readers of the magazine who have written in, perhaps to suggest an interview with their favourite star or a story about a particular topic.

As a top performer, Kylie Minogue will have to give lots of interviews.

7

An editor making a flat-plan.

The editor's job is to choose which of these many suggestions should be included in the magazine. Once the editor has chosen the contents, her or his next task is to make a flat-plan. This is a page-by-page rough outline of the magazine, showing where the stories and features will appear and how much space is to be given to each item. It is a guide both to the writers and to the designers. The writers will be able to see roughly how many words to write for each article. The designers will look at the contents of each page in order to judge how they should arrange the text and pictures.

Regular features appear in the same place in each issue, but adverts and articles must be spaced out as evenly as possible. If readers come across page after page of adverts they will quickly become bored. That is good neither for the editor, nor for the advertisers. The editor will probably lose readers, because they will not buy the next issue. The advertisers will not be pleased because their expensive adverts are not attracting new customers.

If you flick through some of your favourite magazines, you will be able to see how they have been laid out. The editor will hope that he or she has planned the issue so that it is fun to read from the first page to the last. Ask yourself if you would have planned any of the pages differently. Are there too many adverts? Are the features and articles interesting? Do you think that some sections of the magazine appear duller than others? If so, what would you have done instead?

The writers

A weekly magazine usually takes three weeks to produce, from the planning meeting to the day it is published. This time is roughly divided so that each stage – writing, designing and printing – takes about one week to complete.

At the end of the planning meeting the writers will each have been given at least one topic to cover for the next issue. With only seven days at most to finish their articles they have to move fast! In this time they must:

- research the subject of the story to find out as many details about it as possible,
- choose the best way to write the article,
- arrange any interviews that are needed,
- write the article to the right length.

A young writer researches an article for a children's sports magazine.

Once the story is written it is given to the editor. The editor is responsible for everything in the magazine, so it is vital that he or she reads through every item and approves it.

The design stage

When the written pieces are approved, they are passed to the art editor. The art editor is in charge of the team that designs each page of the magazine. The art editor looks at the flat-plan, reads through the text (called the copy) and then tells the designers what kind of style they should use for each piece. The 'look' of each page must give the reader an idea of the mood of the article — for example, whether it is serious or fun.

The design of a magazine is important to its success. A quick glance at any magazine will show you this. The first thing to catch your eye will probably be the pictures. Are they clear, attractive and well-chosen? What about the different sizes and styles of lettering that have been used? These must grab your attention and make the information look interesting. Also, look at the way that different colours are used to match the mood of the feature. All these details can help to attract a reader to a magazine.

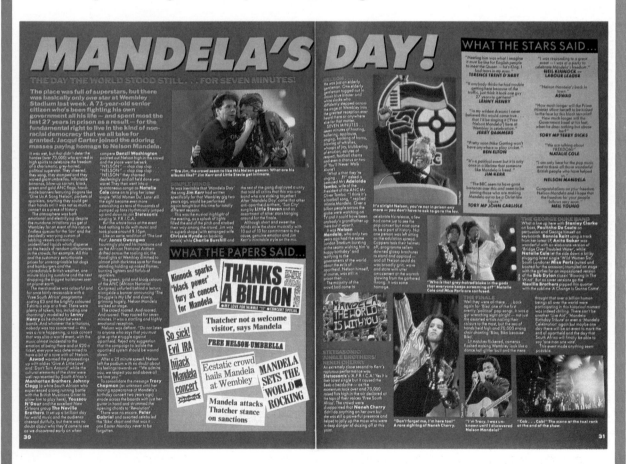

The colours used in this feature on a concert for Nelson Mandela are the colours of the African National Congress.

The designers will now draw up **layouts** for each spread (two facing pages) of the magazine. These layouts show exactly where the text and pictures appear on each page.

Next, the editor will sit down with the art editor to choose the cover picture and the cover design. The cover is

Cover pictures must be attractive and should feature stars such as Jason Donovan.

probably the most important part of any magazine. It should tell you immediately what kind of magazine is on offer and tempt you to pick it up.

The back-up team

The editorial office of a magazine is very busy. Apart from the writers, designers and editors, there are a number of assistants who play a very important back-up role.

- *Editorial assistants* help with a wide variety of jobs, such as answering readers' letters, carrying out research for writers, typing, writing small pieces for the magazine and **proofreading**.
- *Picture researchers* look for the right pictures to go with each article. There are hundreds of picture agencies that keep photographs of different subjects, such as news, sport and fashion. A picture researcher knows exactly where to go to find the right kind of pictures.

Light-boxes are used to help with picture research.

- *Receptionists* answer letters and telephone calls, pass on messages to the editorial team and look after any visitors to the office.

So, the issue has been planned, the writers have come up with a number of interesting stories and features, the picture researchers have found some exciting photographs, and the designers have produced a series of lively and attractive layouts. Now the text and pictures are ready to be sent to production.

But before we go on to look at the production process itself, we will see how a comic is planned and put together.

COMICS AND COMIC MAKERS

TODAY VIDEOS, personal computers, Walkmans and comics are perhaps the favourite forms of entertainment for children. Whereas magazines deal with the 'real world' in a fun and exciting way, comics are concerned purely with the world of the imagination and are filled with fantastic and impossible characters.

Most comics deal with a fantasy world.

13

Not only do comics have a different kind of content to magazines, they look different as well. They are printed on cheaper, rougher paper and use little colour. Because of this they are less expensive to produce than magazines.

The number of people in the editorial office of a comic is much smaller than that of a magazine. Usually there are only a couple of editors at most. One editor plans the contents of the issue and deals with the writers and artists who produce the **comic strips**, while the other will look after the production side. This means dealing with the people who **reproduce** the artwork and print the comic. These editors will have a couple of editorial assistants and a receptionist to help them.

Spiderman is an internationally known comic character.

There is less colour used in this comic than in most children's magazines.

The writers and artists

Most writers and artists who produce strips for comics work 'freelance'. This means that they work for themselves and are 'commissioned' or hired by the comic to provide a strip of a certain number of pages.

The editor is always looking for new writers and artists. Each week he or she will receive many strips and scripts sent in by people wishing to work in comics. Of these, perhaps only one or two of every 100 sent in will have the makings of a good comic strip.

Judging whether or not these 'non-commissioned' strips are good enough is very important for the editor. It is the

Comic artists have to be good at drawing and must have lively imaginations.

main way of spotting new talent. Not only that, he or she must always be planning ahead for the future success of the comic. Readers always want to see new characters and adventures as well as read about their regular favourites.

The first stage in producing a comic strip is to turn a basic idea into a funny or dramatic plot involving strong characters in exciting adventures. When the characters and basic story line have been worked out, the writer will sit down and write a script.

The script describes what is to happen in each **frame** of the strip. It describes the **scenery**, explains what the characters are saying and doing, and details any 'sound effects', (for example Biff! Crash!) that are to be included.

The script is then read by the editor. If the editor wishes any changes to be made, he or she will talk these over with the writer before giving the go-ahead for the artwork to be started.

An artist usually draws each page of the strip 'half-up' – that is, to a size one and a half times bigger than the finished size. This means the artist can get more detail into each frame and also makes the picture look sharper and bolder.

The English editor of 'Teenage Mutant Hero Turtles', Barrie Tomlinson, looks at artwork.

Nowadays, people of all ages read comics.

Because comics used to be aimed just at children, people did not think comic art was very important. However, these days comics are aimed at adults too. Adult comics used to be mostly **science fiction** stories, but now comics are being used to explore serious social, scientific and political subjects. The last few years have also seen the growth in popularity of the 'graphic novel', which is basically a long single story in comic form.

This greater interest in comics has meant that comic art has grown into a serious art form. Many exhibitions of comics are held all over the world each year, with the writers and artists being treated as very important people.

The growth of desk-top publishing has also meant that young artists and writers can produce their own comics quite cheaply. It is a good way for them to see their work in print for the first time, and is a means of gaining popularity for their strips.

The final stage

Once the artwork has been completed, it is passed to a lettering artist who adds the dialogue (words) in speech bubbles. He or she also adds any captions which explain a change of scene or action. Lettering is an art form in itself and it requires expert skill to fit the dialogue and captions into the available space and in a suitable style.

Now the artwork, complete with added speech bubbles and captions, is passed to the editor. He or she will check that it is of the right quality and that there are no mistakes. If all is well, the artwork will be sent to production.

A lettering artist working on a speech bubble.

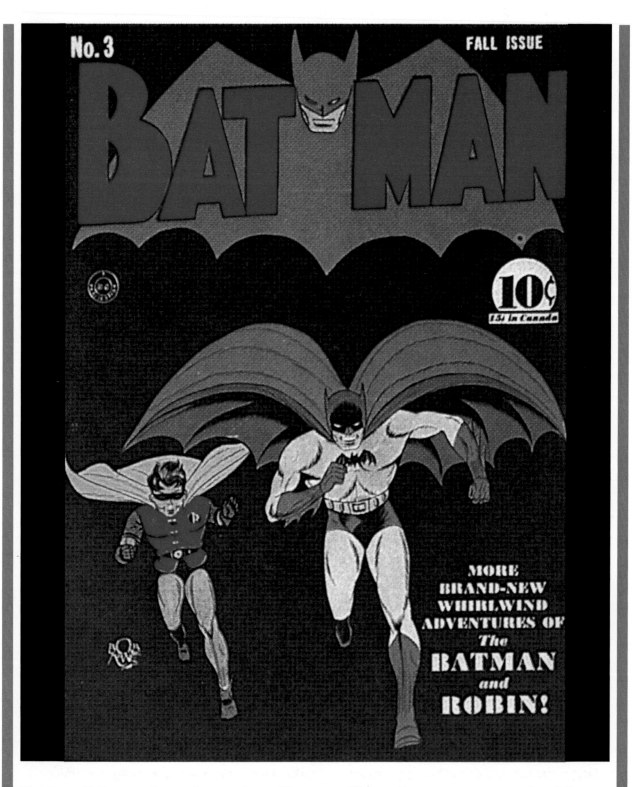

Early editions of comics such as 'Batman' have become very valuable.

PRODUCTION

Magazine production

The editorial department of every magazine has an editor whose job is to look after its production. Production is the turning of the words and pictures supplied by the editorial department into the magazine that you buy in the shops. There are three main stages to this process.

- The copy for each article and feature has to be **typeset**. The pictures have to be reproduced to the right size and to the correct quality.
- The text and pictures have to be fitted together in the way that has been set out in the layouts.
- The pages of the magazine have to be printed and bound.

Typesetters use computers to change copy into the typesize and design that will appear in the magazine. They have to be extremely quick typists.

The production editor acts as a link between the editorial department and the firms that typeset the text, reproduce the pictures and print the magazine. At the start of each issue, the production editor receives a set of timetables, called schedules, from these firms. These schedules set out the dates by which the copy and pictures must be sent to them. The production editor then works out an office schedule for the writers and designers.

ABOVE BPCC Consumer Magazines Ltd use the latest technology to reproduce pictures.

BELOW Magazines being bound at the BPCC factory in East Kilbride, Scotland.

Once the copy has been typeset it is returned to the production editor in the form of pages of printed text, called galleys. The production editor then checks with the designers that the typeset text actually fits in the space that has been allowed for it on the layouts. If it is too long the production editor must cut (edit) it down to the right length. The text then goes back to the typesetters to be re-set.

At the same time the pictures will have been sent to a 'repro-house', which carries out the complicated process of reproducing them to the correct size. The designers will have attached a label to each picture which tells the printers how long and how wide the picture should be printed.

Now the design team will use the galleys and picture proofs to make a paste-up of the layouts. This is where the galleys and proofs are cut up and pasted down on to the layouts in the positions that have been marked by the designers. The paste-up acts as a guide to the printers when the magazine is being printed.

The final stage comes when the printers send proofs of the finished pages to the production editor. These proofs will be checked by both the production editor and the art editor. Once the page proofs have been sent back to the printers, the production editor still cannot relax. He or she is already working on the next issue!

Comic production

There are many types of comic on the market, some of them printed almost totally in black and white, others using full colour strips. Because comics are made up of strips and some short stories and features, their design and production is much simpler than that of magazines.

Notice how the design of these Chinese comics is different from that of comics in the West.

Proofs of artwork from a strip have to be pasted down on grid-sheets in the correct order in which they are to appear in the comic. These layouts act as a guide to the printers.

The strips are sent to a repro-house which returns proofs for the production editor to check. The proofs must be as clear as the original artwork. The text must be easy to read and the pictures must not be blurred or marked.

Once the proofs have been approved, and the galleys for the text have been checked, everything is sent to the printers, along with a copy of the comic's layouts. These show in which order the strips and stories are to appear. The printer makes up page proofs for the production editor, who makes sure that the pages appear in the right order and that the printed pictures are as good as the original artwork. If there are no problems, the page proofs are sent back to the printers and the comic is ready to be printed and bound.

THE SALES PITCH

AS WE have seen, the cost of producing a comic is much lower than that of a magazine. A comic's editorial department is smaller and cheaper to run. The design is simpler, the paper comics are printed on is cheaper and the printing process less complicated.

Adverts in magazines do not necessarily encourage people to buy products. This advert is encouraging girls to do sport.

Magazines cost a lot to produce. Companies cannot make a profit purely on what they charge for the magazines. So, it is important that they persuade as many businesses as possible to pay to advertise their products in the magazine. This is the job of the advertising department.

The advertising department

Different magazines are aimed at different types of readers, for example, children, teenagers and women. These are called the target audiences. Businesses like to advertise their products in magazines because they know that they can reach exactly the kind of person who will want to buy their products.

Let us say that a new magazine called 'Tip Top' is to be brought out. It is to be aimed at people of your age. The advertising department of 'Tip Top' must find some firms to advertise their products and services in the first issue. How do they go about this task?

First of all, they will try to think of as many products as possible that are bought by people in your age group, such as records, books, clothes, videos, drinks, sweets, toys and leisure items like Walkmans and skateboards.

The advertising department also looks at businesses which do not necessarily aim adverts at you. Perhaps a bank or building society could be persuaded to place an advert which describes its services to you, the 'customer of the future'.

These days most large firms use advertising agencies. These agencies specialize in advising firms where to advertise, for example, on television, in the cinema, or on posters, to gain the most **publicity** for their services. The advertising department must persuade these agencies that 'Tip Top' is the best way to reach boys and girls like you.

The advertising department must keep in close contact with the editor. The editor will want to know how much space has been booked for adverts in the next issue. The more adverts that are booked, the bigger the

Magazine producers can afford to print on glossy paper because they get money from advertisers.

In this magazine, an advert for a video of a Kylie Minogue concert in Japan has been placed on the page facing a review of one of her singles.

issue can be. The bigger the issue, the more extra stories and features will have to be written.

The editor also tells the advertising department what kind of articles will be in the issue. It is possible that these articles can be used to attract some more advertisers. For example, an article about Madonna might persuade her record company to place an advert for her latest single or album alongside it.

Magazines earn a great deal of money from selling space for adverts. This money allows the magazine to spend more money on its production. As a result, it will have more features for you to read and it will look glossier and brighter. So you, the reader, do benefit from all this advertising. But what do you think of the adverts themselves? Do you pause to read them? Do they make you buy the products on offer?

The marketing department

What is marketing? It is basically finding out what kind of people buy certain products and why they do so. It also tries to find ways to increase the appeal of these products and therefore increase their sales.

The marketing department of a magazine or comic is concerned with three main areas:

- promotions (free gifts such as posters and badges),
- finding out about the type of people who are regular readers,
- making sure that there are enough copies in the shops.

Promotions attract new readers. It is hoped that these new readers, tempted to buy the magazine or comic through the offer of a free gift, will like its contents so much that they will buy it again. It is important, therefore, that the marketing department produces a promotion that will prove popular.

One way that a marketing department can keep in touch with the likes and interests of the readers is to carry out a reader survey. This is a sheet placed in the magazine or comic from time to time which asks the reader a number of questions such as:

- what do you like about the magazine or comic?
- what don't you like about it?
- what new features would you like to see?
- what are your favourite hobbies?

From this survey, a marketing department can build up a picture of the regular readers. This information is very useful to every department of the magazine or comic.

The marketing department is also responsible for making sure the comics or magazines reach the shops. It plans how many copies are to be printed and aims to sell at least 85 to 90 per cent of them in order to avoid losing money on unsold copies.

ABOVE A selection of promotional material for comics and magazines.

OPPOSITE Children swapping cards given away free in 'Sports Illustrated for Kids'.

MAKING YOUR OWN COMIC STRIP

YOU AND your friends can have a go at making your own comic strips. Have you got an idea which you think would make a good comic strip? It could be a funny story or an adventure. Perhaps you would like to write or draw a science fiction strip or a ghost story. Divide up into small groups and choose who will draw the strip and who will write it.

The first stage is to write the script. First of all, look at some of your favourite comic strips. Study the way these stories are told. Look at how the action develops and the ways that are used to make the reader want to find out what happens next.

It is best to write out in full the story you have thought of. Try to keep it as short and exciting as possible. Then try to pick out the key moments which take the action of your story from one stage to the next. These will be the scenes which will be illustrated in your script. Remember, something new must happen in each frame.

Now decide what your major characters will look like. They will need strong personalities which must come across in the pictures. The next step is to write your detailed script frame by frame. Remember, you must describe what is to appear in each frame and set out what each character will say. You must also include any captions and sound effects that are to appear in the frame.

Finally, the artist among you must try to bring the story to life using as much imagination as she or he can. Vary the size of the frames, choose different angles for each scene and make the special effects look as dramatic as possible. Once again, a close study of your favourite comic strips, such as 'Batman' or 'The Real Ghostbusters', should give you lots of ideas.

ABOVE **This girl is deciding what will happen in each frame of her comic strip.**

OPPOSITE **Some of the most popular comic strips feature animals who act like people.**

GLOSSARY

Comic strips – Stories that appear in comics and that are told in more than one frame.

Designed – The way in which the text and pictures have been arranged on a page.

Frame – A single picture in a comic strip.

Layouts – Pages that show exactly where the text and pictures will appear in the finished comic or magazine.

Marketing – Finding out what kind of people buy particular comics or magazines and discovering ways to attract new readers.

Proofreading – Checking text for mistakes in spelling or grammar.

Publicity – Ways of letting the public know about a product.

Reproduce – To make a copy of an original photograph or piece of artwork for use in a comic or magazine.

Researched – All the facts on a certain subject have been checked.

Scenery – The background against which a story is set, for example in a town or in the country.

Science fiction – A story that is set in space or in the future.

Typeset – To make the words of a story ready to be printed in a comic or magazine.

BOOKS TO READ

How to Draw Cartoons and Caricatures by Judy Tatchell (Usborne, 1987)

Learning the Media by Manuel Alvarado, Robin Gutch and Tana Wollen (Macmillan, 1987)

Magazines by Kim Walden (Wayland, 1988)

Teen Magazines by Tim Merrison (Wayland, 1989)

ACKNOWLEDGEMENTS

The author and Publishers would like to thank the following for providing the illustrations used in this book: BPCC Consumer Magazines Ltd. 20 (top and bottom); Eye Ubiquitous cover, 5, 10, 11, 13, 14, (top and bottom), 18, 21, 26; Trevor Hill 8, 9, 17, 19, 22; London Features International 7; Christine Osborne Pictures 16, 17; Papilio 4, 6, 23, 24, 25, 27, 28, 29; Sefton Picture Library 15; Wayland Picture Library 12.

The author and Publishers would also like to thank BBC Enterprises Limited for permission to use material from 'Fast Forward' and 'Number One', and Independent Television Publications Ltd for permission to use material from 'Look-In'.

Material reproduced from 'The Real Ghostbusters' and Marvel promotional material is reproduced by permission of Marvel Comics Ltd, London, and material from 'Captain America' is reproduced by permission of Marvel Entertainment Group Inc.

INDEX

The numbers in **bold** refer to captions.